AUSTRALIA'S MOST
DEADLY

—

By Karen McGhee

(Australian Geographic logo)

Australian
GEOGRAPHIC

AUSTRALIA'S MOST
DEADLY

Australia's Most Deadly is published by Australian Geographic, an imprint of Bauer Media Ltd. All images and text are copyright © Bauer Media and may not be reproduced without the written permission of the publishers.

First published in 2014 by:

MEDIA GROUP

Bauer Media
54 Park Street, Sydney, NSW 2000
Telephone (02) 9263 9813
Email editorial@ausgeo.com.au

www.australiangeographic.com.au

Australian Geographic customer service:
1300 555 176 (local call rate within Australia).
From overseas +61 2 8667 5295

Text Karen McGhee
Book design Mike Rossi
Picture research Jess Teideman
Print production Chris Clear
Editor Lauren Smith
Sub-editors Carolyn Barry, John Pickrell
Managing Director Matthew Stanton
Publishing Director - Specialist Division Brendon Hill
Publisher Jo Runciman
Editor-in-Chief, Australian Geographic Chrissie Goldrick

Printed in China by Leo Paper Products

This list was kindly provided by the
Australian Museum, Sydney NSW
www.australianmuseum.net.au

RELATED TITLES:

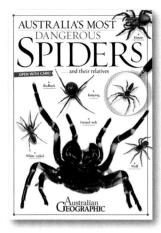

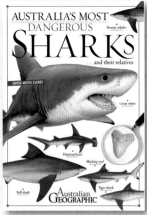

AUSTRALIA'S MOST
DEADLY

All of the animals listed in this book have been given a deadly factor out of 10 – the higher the score, the more deadly the animal! The Australian Museum in Sydney developed this ranking system, and the score given to a species is based on the threat it poses to you, combined with the odds of encountering it. This means that our number one most deadly animal might not be the one you were expecting...

CREATURES THAT CAN KILL YOU!

CONTENTS

YOU'RE ON THE MENU!

There's not much you can do if one of these huge creatures wants to makes a meal of you!

SALTWATER CROCODILE

Saltwater crocodiles haven't changed much since the time of the dinosaurs, more than 65 million years ago. And why would they? They are among nature's most effective killing machines.

DEADLY FACTOR:

8/10

WARNING
ACHTUNG 警告

SAFETY TIPS

The best advice when it comes to crocs is stay away from them! If you venture into saltwater crocodile territory, you won't stand a chance. These reptiles can lurk, staying deadly still, hidden underwater for more than an hour at a time, and when they strike they move at lightning speed.

WHERE DO I LIVE?

CROC SPOTS ▶

Saltwater crocs are found in the freshwater river systems and coastlines of northern Australia. Mangrove swamps and riverbanks are their favourite attack zones, but they've even been spotted kilometres out to sea.

FACT BOX — The Death Roll

Each year 1-2 people are killed by crocodiles in northern Australia and there are 4-10 non-fatal attacks. When they strike a large animal – such as a human – crocodiles usually grab a head or limb and then roll in the water. This will either break their prey's neck or drown it.

Did you know?

Crocodile babies are just 25cm long when they hatch. But males can grow to more than 6m and weigh a tonne. There are unverified reports of crocs up to 8m long!

MAN-EATING SHARKS

Very few shark species deserve the label 'man-killer', but there are some rare exceptions. These three shark species are responsible for most attacks on people in Australia and around the world.

▶ BULL SHARK

DEADLY FACTOR: 8/10

Distribution, 'personality' and size combine to make this **predator** the most fearsome shark in Australian waters. It hunts where we swim – around the coast and in harbours and bays. Unlike other sharks, it even swims up into freshwater rivers. Adults grow to a length of more than 3m, meaning they can easily handle a human. The bull shark's reputation is sealed by its aggressive nature and omnivorous diet. When hunting it will have a go at eating just about anything edible in the water.

WHERE DO I LIVE?

Did you know?

Bull sharks have been known to attack and kill people swimming in waist-deep water.

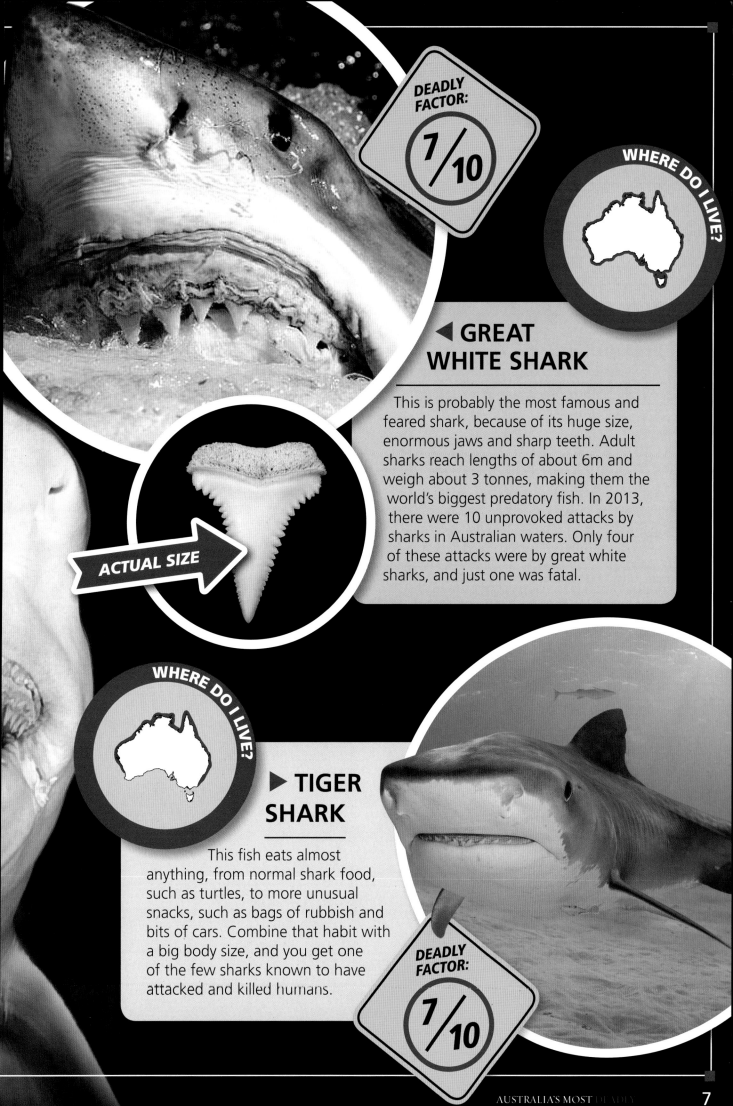

DEADLY FACTOR: 7/10

WHERE DO I LIVE?

◀ GREAT WHITE SHARK

This is probably the most famous and feared shark, because of its huge size, enormous jaws and sharp teeth. Adult sharks reach lengths of about 6m and weigh about 3 tonnes, making them the world's biggest predatory fish. In 2013, there were 10 unprovoked attacks by sharks in Australian waters. Only four of these attacks were by great white sharks, and just one was fatal.

ACTUAL SIZE

WHERE DO I LIVE?

▶ TIGER SHARK

This fish eats almost anything, from normal shark food, such as turtles, to more unusual snacks, such as bags of rubbish and bits of cars. Combine that habit with a big body size, and you get one of the few sharks known to have attacked and killed humans.

DEADLY FACTOR: 7/10

VENOMOUS BITES!

We can't hide it - Australia definitely has a lot of potentially deadly biters!

BLUE-RINGED OCTOPUS

Normally, these small marine creatures don't stand out. But when they're startled or threatened, they darken and start to pulse with glowing circles of shimmering blue.

SMALL BUT DEADLY

These are the world's most lethal octopuses. These deadly creatures are usually perfectly camouflaged for hiding out in rock pools. But when they start to pulse, it's a clear warning sign to predators to stay away. Unfortunately, it's also a fascinating colour that often makes people want to pick them up. They bite, but it barely leaves a mark and is usually so painless it goes unnoticed. Within as little as 10 minutes the victim can feel a prickling, followed by numbness. Soon the victim has difficulty breathing and swallowing, and is left fighting for their life.

DEADLY FACTOR:

7 / 10

WHERE DO I LIVE?

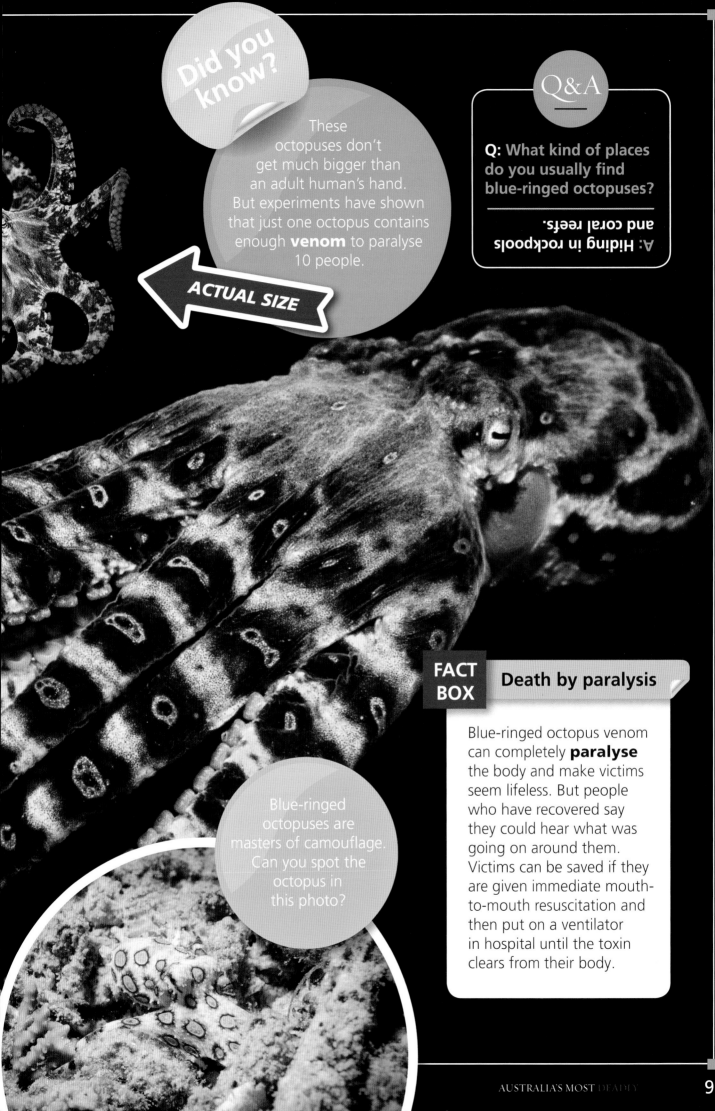

These octopuses don't get much bigger than an adult human's hand. But experiments have shown that just one octopus contains enough **venom** to paralyse 10 people.

ACTUAL SIZE

Q: What kind of places do you usually find blue-ringed octopuses?

A: Hiding in rockpools and coral reefs.

Blue-ringed octopuses are masters of camouflage. Can you spot the octopus in this photo?

FACT BOX   **Death by paralysis**

Blue-ringed octopus venom can completely **paralyse** the body and make victims seem lifeless. But people who have recovered say they could hear what was going on around them. Victims can be saved if they are given immediate mouth-to-mouth resuscitation and then put on a ventilator in hospital until the toxin clears from their body.

SLITHERING SNAKES

Each year up to 3000 people are bitten by snakes in Australia! These days, because of effective antivenoms, usually only one or two snakebite victims die a year.

WHERE DO I LIVE?

▶ EASTERN BROWN SNAKE

No other snake species bites or kills more people in Australia than the eastern brown. Brown snake venom contains an exceptionally strong fast-acting nerve toxin, though compared to many other snakes, their small fangs don't inject much venom when they bite. This is the snake you're most likely to come in contact with in Australia, and is a fast-moving and agile snake that becomes aggressive when cornered - so be careful if you meet one!

DEADLY FACTOR:

8 / 10

FACT BOX **Snakebite ID tip**

A polyvalent **antivenom** is now available – it works on the bites of all Australian snakes, though it is still best to use the antivenom specifically designed for each species. You should never wash a snakebite wound because the venom left around it can be used to identify the type of snake that caused the injury.

◀ COMMON DEATH ADDER

This snake has such toxic venom that it's on the list of the top 10 deadliest snakes in the world! Death adders don't move about much but lie hidden, waiting for prey. They have one of the fastest strikes of any snake, and are a common hazard for bushwalkers.

DEADLY FACTOR:

7/10

WHERE DO I LIVE?

▶ DUGITE (SPOTTED BROWN SNAKE)

This highly venomous snake is active during the daytime and often seen around urban and semi-rural areas. The species is particularly well-known to Perth residents – it's responsible for three-quarters of all snakebite admissions to hospitals in the area. Without antivenom, there's a high chance that a bite can be fatal – though the actual bite itself is said to be almost painless, with no real swelling.

WHERE DO I LIVE?

DEADLY FACTOR:

7/10

◀ BLUE-BELLIED BLACK SNAKE

This snake doesn't just bite – it will have a good chew, which lets it inject as much venom as possible! It prefers to avoid any confrontation. When that's not an option, it becomes extremely aggressive, hisses loudly and flattens out its body to make itself look larger.

WHERE DO I LIVE?

DEADLY FACTOR:

6/10

▼ COASTAL TAIPAN

WHERE DO I LIVE?

The coastal taipan snake is the third most toxic snake in the world, and it has the longest fangs of any Australian snake – about 13mm long, so it can deliver a serious bite. Before the introduction of its antivenom in 1956, taipan bites were nearly always fatal – in severe cases, death can occur in just 30 minutes. An extremely alert and nervous creature, it prefers to avoid confrontation, but puts up a ferocious defence if it's cornered or surprised. First it stops still, and then hurls its lightweight body forward.

DEADLY FACTOR:

7 / 10

Did you know?

This snake's venom is specially designed for warm-blooded creatures and adult taipans only eat mammals and birds. Taipans release their prey after they bite. They know their venom will kill quickly anyway and it means the snake won't be harmed in a struggle.

▼ MULGA (KING BROWN)

This snake's biggest claim to fame is that it produces more venom than any other snake in the world when it bites. It can deliver a massive 150mg of venom when it strikes – as much as four times more than other venomous snakes. When they bite, they hang on and chew!

WHERE DO I LIVE?

DEADLY FACTOR:

7 / 10

▲ COLLETT'S SNAKE

The Collett's snake is a close relative of the very widespread mulga snake, and the bites of both snakes cause a similar range of extreme symptoms – these include a nightmarish combination of stomach aches, diarrhoea, **nausea**, vomiting and headaches.

DEADLY FACTOR:

6 / 10

WHERE DO I LIVE?

▶ HIGHLAND COPPERHEAD

The highland copperhead, one of three copperhead species found in Australia, prefers to live at high altitudes. These snakes have been responsible for a few deaths, and these have been because of the paralysis caused by the venom. Muscle damage and mild bleeding are also symptoms of a copperhead bite.

DEADLY FACTOR:

6 / 10

WHERE DO I LIVE?

RED-BELLIED BLACK SNAKE ▼

Compared to other venomous snakes, this is a placid creature that will usually move out of your way. It can deliver a nasty bite, with a powerful venom that can make you very sick. It's one of the few venomous snakes still found in the Sydney region.

WHERE DO I LIVE?

DEADLY FACTOR:

7/10

WHERE DO I LIVE?

▼ **INLAND TAIPAN**

A high-potency mix of killer compounds make the inland taipan the world's most venomous snake – but it's not the most dangerous. That's because this snake lives only in a very isolated part of the country, and also has a shy and laid-back temperament.

WHERE DO I LIVE?

◄

YELLOW-BELLIED SEA SNAKE

The yellow-bellied sea snake lives its entire life in the ocean! This snake is highly venomous, with venom that contains potent nerve and muscle **toxins.** Luckily it only has tiny fangs – about 1.5 mm long – and its bite doesn't deliver a lot of venom. So far, no deaths have been reported in Australia, though it has killed people overseas.

DEADLY FACTOR:

6/10

▶ TIGER SNAKE

On average, tiger snakes kill about one person a year. It's because they occur close to where lots of people live, including some parts of suburban Melbourne, that they are responsible for Australia's second-highest number of snakebites. Before a tiger snake antivenom was developed in the 1930s, almost half of all people bitten by these snakes would die.

WHERE DO I LIVE?

DEADLY FACTOR:

7 / 10

DEADLY FACTOR:

6 / 10

Did you know?

Male red-bellied blacks are known to travel extensively during the mating season, looking for females. So you should watch out for them particularly during spring. They are also known to love basking in the sunshine.

KILLER SPIDERS

Australia has some truly terrifying spiders lurking around. What makes these particular eight-legged killers even more scary is that they live in some of our most populated areas!

DEADLY FACTOR:

8/10

Males, with a 25mm-long body, are smaller than females, which grow about 10mm longer. But males have more potent venom.

DEADLY FACTOR:

6/10

WHERE DO I LIVE?

◀ REDBACK

Male redbacks are tiny, just a few millimetres long, and mostly go unnoticed. Females have a body that's about 1cm long and is recognisable by the red stripe on its back that gives the species its name. No deaths have been recorded since antivenom became available in the 1950s. There are still about 2000 bites each year, and about 250 of these are bad enough to need the redback antivenom. A bad bite from a redback can have very serious effects, including severe and persistent pain.

True or False?

The fangs of a funnel-web spider are hollow.

A: True

◀ SYDNEY FUNNEL-WEB

The Sydney funnel-web's is the world's deadliest spider. If you have the misfortune of encountering one, it will put on a fierce attack display lifting up its body, front legs and huge fangs as it prepares to lunge. Then it will thrust down frighteningly fast with fangs that are big enough to stab through a toenail. It has a highly toxic, fast-acting venom that killed at least 13 people between 1927 and 1980. Fortunately, no-one has died since an antivenom became available in 1981.

WHERE DO I LIVE?

Q: How long is a funnel-web's fang?

A: About 6mm long.

WHAT IS AUSTRALIA'S DEADLIEST ANIMAL?

TOP **30** KILLERS

START HERE!

| ○ INSECTS | ○ ARACHNIDS | ○ MOLLUSCS | ○ STINGERS | ○ FISH | ○ REPTILES |

30

GIANT CENTIPEDE

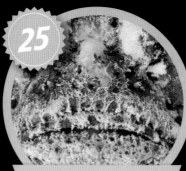

25

REEF STONEFISH

24

REDBACK SPIDER

29

BULL ANT

26

SMOOTH TOADFISH

23

INLAND TAIPAN

28

AUSTRALIAN PARALYSIS TICK

27

BLUE-BELLIED BLACK SNAKE

22

HIGHLAND COPPERHEAD

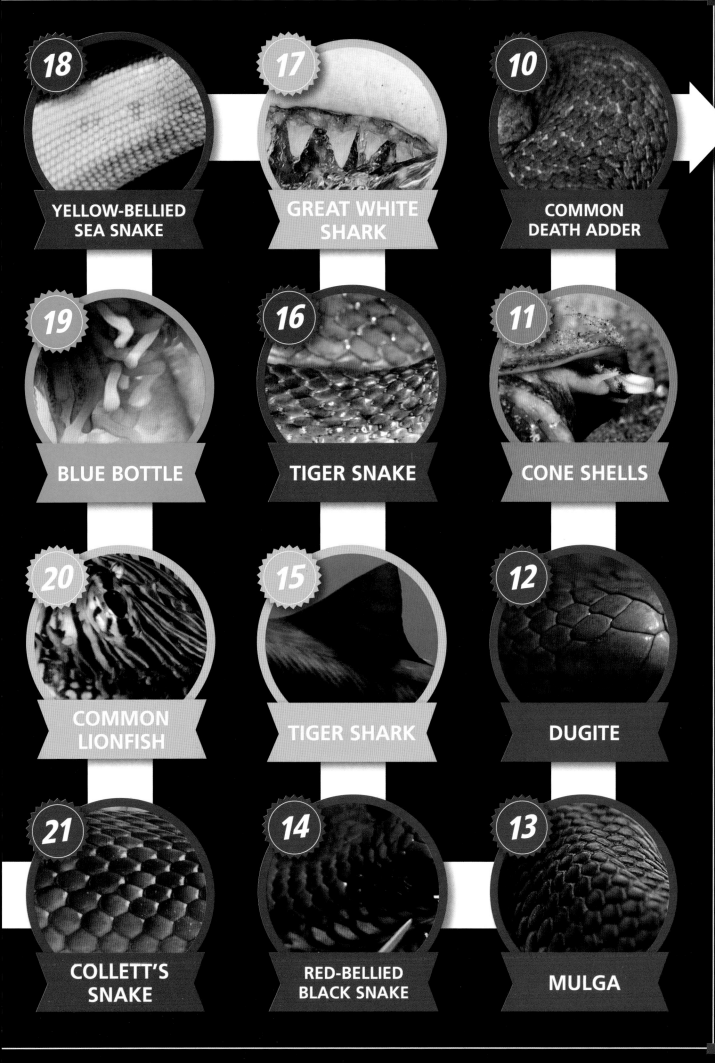

18 YELLOW-BELLIED SEA SNAKE

17 GREAT WHITE SHARK

10 COMMON DEATH ADDER

19 BLUE BOTTLE

16 TIGER SNAKE

11 CONE SHELLS

20 COMMON LIONFISH

15 TIGER SHARK

12 DUGITE

21 COLLETT'S SNAKE

14 RED-BELLIED BLACK SNAKE

13 MULGA

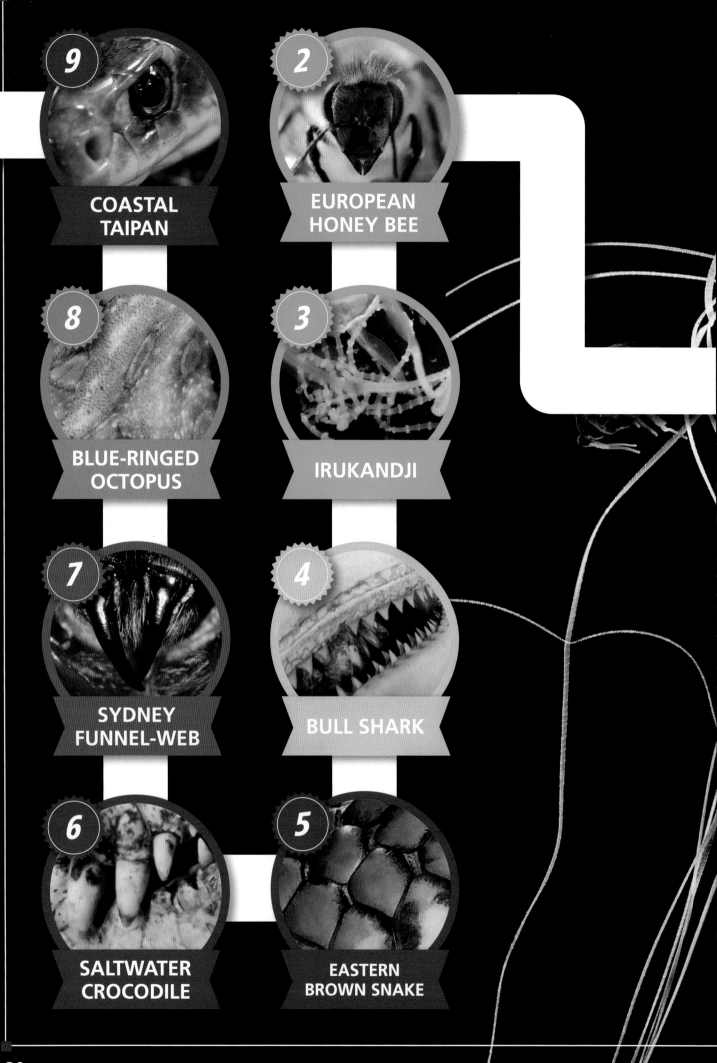

9 COASTAL TAIPAN

2 EUROPEAN HONEY BEE

8 BLUE-RINGED OCTOPUS

3 IRUKANDJI

7 SYDNEY FUNNEL-WEB

4 BULL SHARK

6 SALTWATER CROCODILE

5 EASTERN BROWN SNAKE

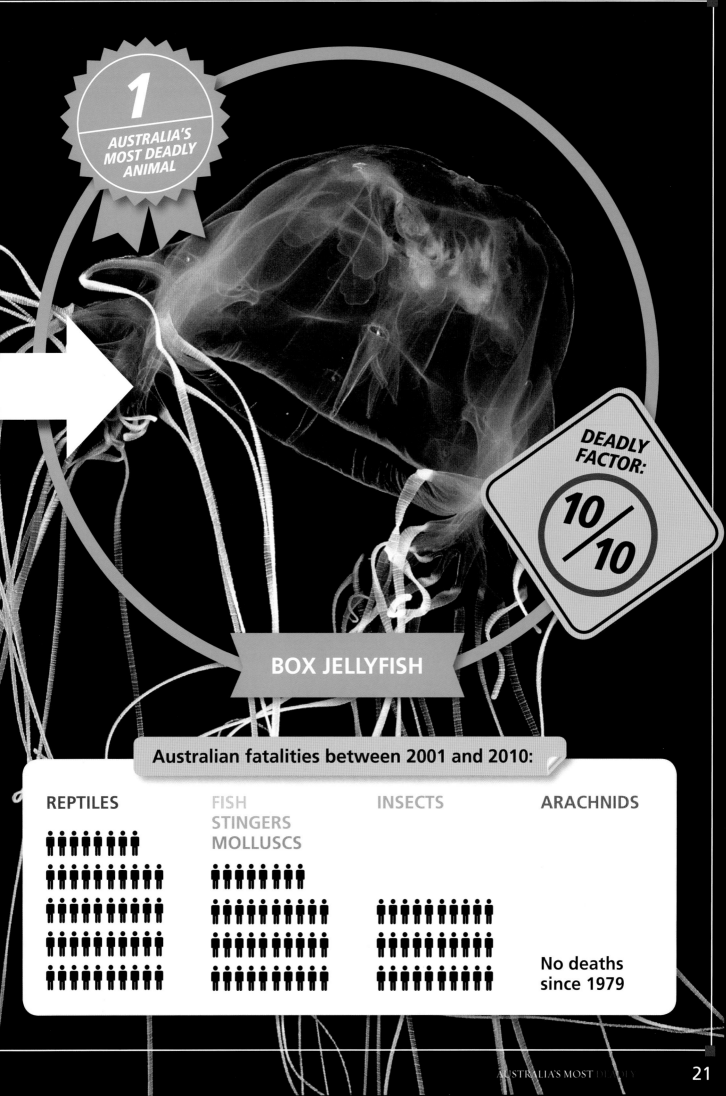

1
AUSTRALIA'S
MOST DEADLY
ANIMAL

DEADLY
FACTOR:
10 / 10

BOX JELLYFISH

Australian fatalities between 2001 and 2010:

REPTILES	FISH STINGERS MOLLUSCS	INSECTS	ARACHNIDS
👤👤👤👤👤👤👤👤			
👤👤👤👤👤👤👤👤👤👤	👤👤👤👤👤👤👤👤		
👤👤👤👤👤👤👤👤👤👤	👤👤👤👤👤👤👤👤👤👤	👤👤👤👤👤👤👤👤👤👤	
👤👤👤👤👤👤👤👤👤👤	👤👤👤👤👤👤👤👤👤👤	👤👤👤👤👤👤👤👤👤👤	
👤👤👤👤👤👤👤👤👤👤	👤👤👤👤👤👤👤👤👤👤	👤👤👤👤👤👤👤👤👤👤	No deaths since 1979

None of these creatures want to hurt you,
but they might just kill you by accident.

FATAL FISH

There are other deadly fish in our seas as well as our giant sharks. These
odd-looking fish mightn't seem as vicious, but they pack a serious punch!

Did you know?

Lionfish
are aggressive
and territorial.
They'll point their
poisonous spines at
a threat and swim
towards it.

DEADLY FACTOR:

6/10

WHERE DO I LIVE?

DEADLY FACTOR:

6/10

◀ COMMON LIONFISH

The bright red on this species is a telltale warning sign that it's dangerous! It has 17 poisonous spines that it uses against both predators and prey. And though lionfish have not yet been known to have caused deaths in Australia, people have been stung. It's said to be exceptionally painful. In the worst cases the venom can cause **hallucinations**, paralysis and heart failure. Those most at risk are scuba divers and snorkellers.

▲ REEF STONEFISH

This weird-looking fish has a sting so excruciating that the pain can cause muscle weakness, paralysis and shock - these factors may even lead to death! They have amazing camouflage that makes them blend in perfectly amongst reef rubble, so people often make the mistake of stepping on one. It has 13 **poisonous** spines on its back and these are so tough they can pierce shoes as well as the feet inside. It raises these upwards when it's disturbed.

WHERE DO I LIVE?

DEADLY FACTOR:

6/10

◀ SMOOTH TOADFISH

Fry a fillet of the smooth toadfish and it's likely to be your last meal! Parts of the body of this pufferfish (it's liver, ovaries, intestines and skin) are very poisonous when eaten, for humans and animals! One study recorded 11 pufferfish poisoning cases in just over a year in New South Wales alone.

WHERE DO I LIVE?

BOX JELLYFISH

Serious stings from a box jellyfish can cause death before paramedics even have a chance to administer the antivenom.

WHERE DO I LIVE?

SERIAL KILLER

This is one of the deadliest creatures on the planet. Its fast-acting venom can kill an adult in less than five minutes. Each year it kills an estimated 100 people worldwide – more than crocodiles, sharks and stonefish combined. In Australia alone, box jellies have killed at least 64 people since the first recorded death in 1883. Their stinging cells work like high-pressured syringes, plunging into human skin and leaving life-long scars in survivors. You're most at risk of meeting a box jelly in coastal waters across northern Australia between October and June.

DEADLY FACTOR: 10/10

1ST AUSTRALIA'S MOST DEADLY ANIMAL

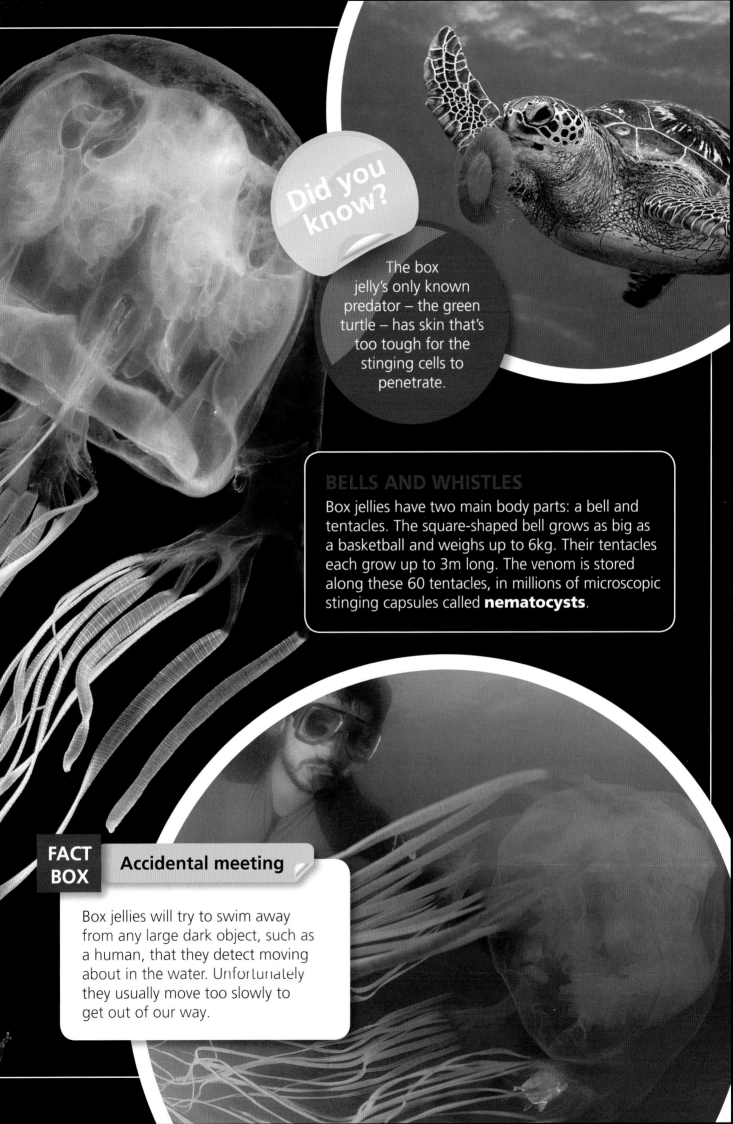

The box jelly's only known predator – the green turtle – has skin that's too tough for the stinging cells to penetrate.

BELLS AND WHISTLES

Box jellies have two main body parts: a bell and tentacles. The square-shaped bell grows as big as a basketball and weighs up to 6kg. Their tentacles each grow up to 3m long. The venom is stored along these 60 tentacles, in millions of microscopic stinging capsules called **nematocysts**.

FACT BOX

Accidental meeting

Box jellies will try to swim away from any large dark object, such as a human, that they detect moving about in the water. Unfortunately they usually move too slowly to get out of our way.

STINGERS
OF THE SEA

Jellyfish and bluebottles can't get out of your way so, if you know they're about, stay clear of the water.

DEADLY FACTOR:

9/10

WHERE DO I LIVE?

◄ IRUKANDJI

This jellyfish is tiny, with a bell about 2cm wide, and tentacles up to 50cm long. Don't let its size deceive you! It causes one of nature's most excruciatingly awful experiences – irukandji syndrome! Each year more than 60 people across northern Australia are hospitalised in agonising pain with this condition. Most people don't notice when they're stung, but about half an hour later, the victim develops severe backache, followed by a headache and agonising pain through the muscles.

FACT BOX **Crazy brave**

Australian doctor Jack Barnes deliberately stung himself, his son and a willing surf lifesaver with this jellyfish in 1964. He wanted to test whether it caused irukandji syndrome. It did! All three ended up in hospital – and the stinger responsible was named *Carukia barnesi*, after the doctor.

ACTUAL SIZE

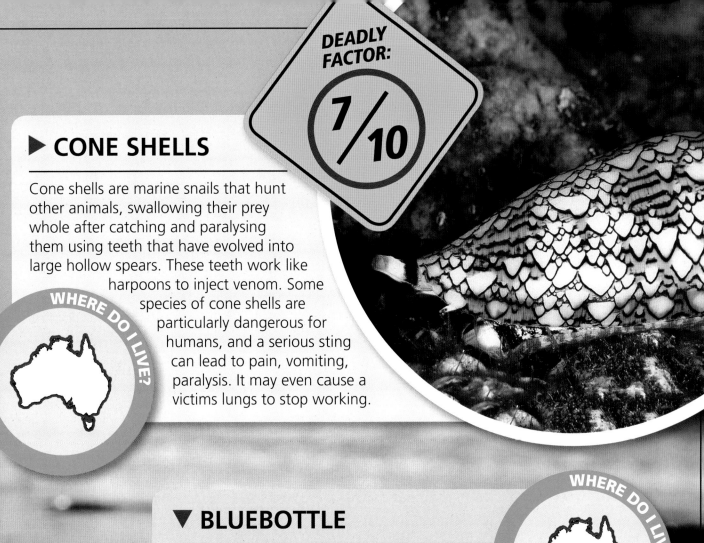

▶ CONE SHELLS

Cone shells are marine snails that hunt other animals, swallowing their prey whole after catching and paralysing them using teeth that have evolved into large hollow spears. These teeth work like harpoons to inject venom. Some species of cone shells are particularly dangerous for humans, and a serious sting can lead to pain, vomiting, paralysis. It may even cause a victims lungs to stop working.

WHERE DO I LIVE?

▼ BLUEBOTTLE

Bluebottles are the most common cause of marine stings in Australia. Bluebottles aren't jellyfish – each one is a connected colony of different animals, relying on each other for survival. One part is the float, another part is for feeding and there's a part that reproduces. The bit to worry about is the tentacle. That can be almost 3m long and is covered in stinging cells. Although rare, deaths have been recorded. Usually, the intense burning sensation stops after an hour or two.

WHERE DO I LIVE?

Did you know?

Even when bluebottles are dead, their stinging cells can still work. So never touch them, even when you see them lying on the beach.

Most of these creatures would prefer not to sting us, but sometimes they have no choice.

EUROPEAN HONEY BEE

This busy, buzzing little bee seems harmless, and it is for most of us – but for 700,000 Australians, it can be a deadly killer.

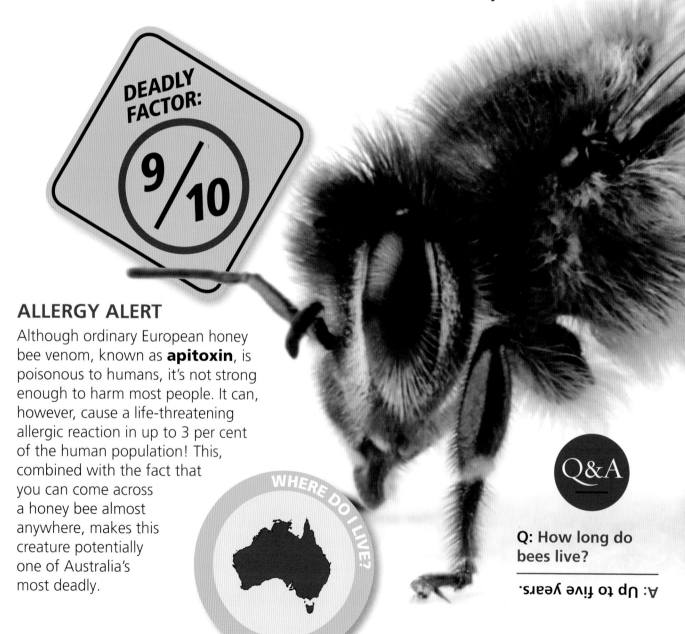

DEADLY FACTOR: 9/10

ALLERGY ALERT

Although ordinary European honey bee venom, known as **apitoxin**, is poisonous to humans, it's not strong enough to harm most people. It can, however, cause a life-threatening allergic reaction in up to 3 per cent of the human population! This, combined with the fact that you can come across a honey bee almost anywhere, makes this creature potentially one of Australia's most deadly.

WHERE DO I LIVE?

Q&A

Q: How long do bees live?

A: Up to five years.

SUDDEN SHOCKS

A bee sting is painful for anyone and most of us will be stung once or twice during our lives. But a person who's allergic to bee venom can develop symptoms of **anaphylactic shock** within minutes of being stung. Their airways swell and become blocked. Their blood pressure drops dramatically and without medical attention they can die.

Did you know?

Only female bees – workers and queens – have stings: they're connected to venom sacs on their abdomens.

FIRST AID

A life-threatening allergic reaction may need to be treated with an injection of **adrenalin**.

FACT BOX — Group warning

Even for the average person who isn't allergic to apitoxin, a swarm of honey bees can be a danger. It's estimated that the jabs of about 500 bees would contain enough poison to kill a non-allergic person.

INFERNAL INSECTS

The first rule with these insects is to stay clear. If you are bitten or stung, it's important that you know your first aid, and don't panic!

▶ GIANT CENTIPEDE

DEADLY FACTOR: 5/10

The bite of this multi-legged mini-beast can be intensely painful for several days. But, thankfully, no one has yet been known to die from it. They bite using a large pair of sideways-moving fangs that are really modified legs, known as 'forcipules'. They contain poison glands, found just behind the head. They grow up to 14cm long. Never poke them with a stick! Their many legs are each tipped with claws, making them exceptionally good climbers.

WHERE DO I LIVE?

Did you know?

Centipede mothers are devoted parents that guard their eggs and hatchlings by curling their bodies around them.

◀ AUSTRALIAN PARALYSIS TICK

DEADLY FACTOR: 5/10

Most people only have a mild reaction to a paralysis tick bite. In some people, though, it's so severe it can be fatal. When they bite us, they remain attached for a few days feeding on our blood for protein. When they attach, they're just 3mm long. As they fill up on our blood, they swell to more than five times that size. After a few days, when they're full, they drop off.

WHERE DO I LIVE?

▶ JACK JUMPER ANT

DEADLY FACTOR: 5/10

This carnivorous, **scavenging** insect is a large black and orange ant with a potentially fatal sting. Its venom isn't deadly to most people, though it makes the sting very painful. A very small number of people have an allergic reaction to it. In severe cases, victims can suffer an anaphylactic shock, which can be fatal. On average, these ants kill someone about once every four years.

WHERE DO I LIVE?

Glossary

adrenalin	A chemical produced by a person or animal to make their body ready to fight or run.
anaphylactic shock	An extreme and sometimes deadly allergic reaction.
antivenom	A medicine that can block venom from harming a human.
apitoxin	A poison produced by honey bees.
hallucinations	Visual sensations that are not real.
nausea	The sick feeling when you want to vomit.
nematocysts	Specialised cells in a jellyfish (or one of its relatives) that contain a barbed sting.
paralyse	Make unable to feel or move.
poisonous	Full of, or containing, a toxin that is harmful for the victim.
predator	An animal that hunts and eats other animals.
scavenging	Hunting for and eating other animals that have already died.
toxins	Poisons produced by plants or animals.
venom	A poison that an animal produces and injects into another animal.

FURTHER READING

Australia's Most Dangerous
2007, Australian Geographic

Dangerous Animals
Karin Cox & Steve Parish
2010, Steve Parish Publishing

Dangerous Australians
2006, Penguin

Dangerous Aussie animals
Lindsay Marsh
2010, Ready-Ed Publications